Mathematical Reasoning

FOR SELECTIVE SCHOOL TESTS, OPPORTUNITY CLASS TESTS AND PROBLEM SOLVING

BOOK 3

Mohan Dhall

Five Senses Education *Pty* Ltd
2/195 Prospect Highway
Seven Hills 2147
New South Wales
Australia

First Published 2023

Dhall, Mohan
Mathematical Reasoning – Book 3

ISBN 978-1-76032-489-6

Contents

Foreword

Mathematical reasoning skills are an aspect of critical thinking. Critical thinking is an essential skill that students need to develop. Mathematical reasoning requires students to be able to work numerically, understand number relationships, understand mathematical operations, see patterns, transpose, extrapolate, do graphical interpretation, understand data represented in concrete and abstract forms, understand spatial relationships and representations, calculate the probability of an event or events occurring, and use known data to calculate unknown data.

Developing mathematical reasoning is necessary for making informed decisions in everyday life: comparing prices of packages with different weights, understanding weights and measurements when mixing food, or understanding ratios and volumes when mixing paint and colour.

In a rapidly changing world, characterised by multiple and competing information sources, developing mathematical reasoning skills and the ability to reason logically has never been more important. Mathematical reasoning is a fundamental life skill for a meaningful life.

Practice on the problems in this book will help students to develop a range of mathematical reasoning skills. Prior to practising, students should read through the section at the start which provides strategies. Using these strategies will be helpful to developing the skills required to think through complex problems.

About the author

Mohan Dhall is an experienced teacher and teacher-educator, author and educational manager. Trained in gifted education, Mohan has developed many critical thinking courses for students and has also trained teachers in critical and creative thinking skills. As Director, he ran one of Australia's longest running school based centres for gifted children. He has written hundreds of different types of critical thinking questions and had more than 70 books published. Mohan is currently the Academic Leader of M2K Education and Advisory.

Mathematical reasoning - an introduction

Mathematical reasoning involves the application and the development of a number of different thinking skills. Aspects of critical thinking include skills involving each of the following:

- analysis
- comparing
- generalising
- estimation
- justification
- grouping and ordering
- abstracting
- adding, subtracting, multiplying and dividing
- identifying patterns and numerical relationships
- understanding symbolic representations
- explaining
- describing
- identifying.

An essential aspect of mathematical reasoning is logic. Logic is an application of the principles of reasoning to evidence or data. Two important aspects of logical reasoning are deductive reasoning and inductive reasoning.

Deductive reasoning
This type of thinking requires a person to be able to draw valid or certain conclusions from a premise or premises and the application of defined rules.

Inductive reasoning
This type of thinking requires a person to be able to draw general conclusions from the premises but may not be certain. The generalisation should be plausible, but it will not be certain.

Students may find that they are distracted by generalisations that are plausible but are not assured.

General strategies for dealing with different questions

When presented with mathematical information, rules and data, it is important to keep a clear mind about what the problem requires and what information, facts and relationships have been given. A strategy for dealing with complicated information is to write down, in shortened notation, what has been given.

Other strategies include:

1. Reading ALL of the information provided before answering the question.
2. If there is information given in bullet points – such as Statements - then as you read each statement ask yourself, "is this true? Does this make sense?"
3. Read ALL of the answers before making a selection.
4. Even if you think the answer is A or B complete reading ALL of the answers prior to making your selection.
5. If there is graphical data, look at the title of the graph, and the label on each axis before you start your analysis. Carefully look at the scale as well so you know what the values represented are. Note that a graph can have three axes (left, right and horizontal).
6. Be prepared to keep more than one piece of information in your mind at a time. You will need to do this when there are different rules applied to information.
7. DO NOT use your general knowledge to answer any of the questions. All the information you need is in the question. No extraneous information should be required to successfully answer the questions.
8. Identify the type of question being asked so that you know what thinking skills you will be utilising.
9. If there is visual stimulus look at it carefully and try and determine the relationships between the relevant parts of the stimulus.
10. Use estimation as a time saver. Often a quick estimation will help.
11. If you do not 'see information' then practise reading to yourself out loud. You can also underline key words in data to retain it.
12. There can be two or three steps required so make sure you complete a question to the end, not answering it before the final calculation has been made.
13. If you are unsure, experiment. It is okay to try a few combinations as you work your way through a mathematical problem. Baulking and giving up does not solve problems or create resilience.

Mathematical Reasoning Problems

Question 1

Half of the people are right a third of the time. There are 168 decisions to be made during the year.

How many decisions do these people get wrong?

A. 24

B. 28

C. 48

D. 140

E. 144

Question 2

18 people survived the bridge accident where 162 perished

Which of the following **cannot** be considered a lucky number used by a survivor?

A. $^1/_{18}$

B. 1

C. 9

D. 0.1

E. 12

Question 3

Of the prime numbers between 10 and 100 what is the difference between those with digits that add to a square number and those with digits that add to a prime number?

A. 10

B. 7

C. 6

D. 5

E. 4

Question 4

Which of the following **cannot** be an answer to this this pattern?

1 + 4 = 5
2 + 5 = 12
3 + 6 = 21
8 + 11 = ?

A. 96

B. 40

C. 52

D. 92

E. 42

Question 5

In a code, 2.10.2 is 2 pm and 1.9.3 is 1 pm.

Which of these is 10 pm?

A. 5.0.5

B. 4.6.4

C. 9.4.9

D. 8.8.8

E. 3.7.3

Question 6

An analogue clock gains two hours every one hour of actual time. In a complete 24-hour period how many times will it show the correct time, assuming it is correct at midnight (the start of the day).

A. 2

B. 3

C. 4

D. 5

E. 6

Question 7

Look at the figure below.

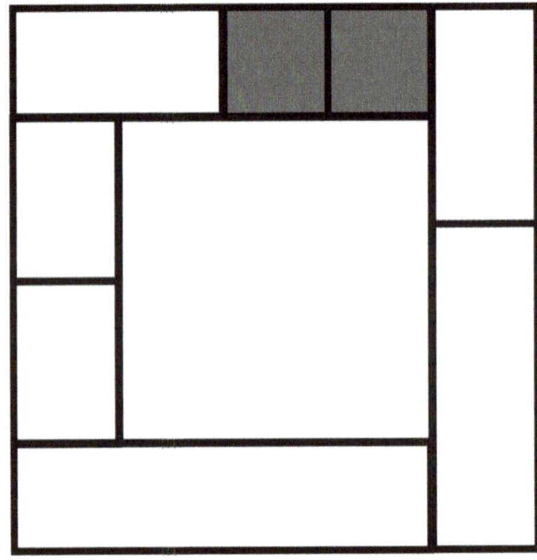

What proportion of this shape is coloured?

A. $^1/_{15}$

B. $^2/_{25}$

C. $^1/_{18}$

D. $^1/_{12}$

E. $^1/_{16}$

Question 8

Mumela was born on 9th September 1961. Her siblings were born on 1st January 1963, 24th June 1964, 5th November 1965 and 13th January 1967.

How many days after Mumela was born was her last sibling born?

A. 1948

B. 1924

C. 1952

D. 1984

E. 1962

Question 9

Lester, Brintu and Kanav each think of a different whole number that is greater than 40 and less than 100.

- Lester's number is a multiple of 7.
- Brintu's number is an even number which is a multiple of 9.
- Kanav's number is an odd number between 71 and 90

What is the difference between the largest possible value of Kanav's number and the largest difference between Lester and Brintu's numbers?

A. 41

B. 42

C. 43

D. 45

E. 47

Question 10

Coyne had $50.

He gave half of his money to Albert. He gave some money to Misty. He then gave one third of what was left to Floyd. Floyd gave a quarter of what he was given to Rajeev. Rajeev got $1.50.

How much money did Coyne give to Misty?

A. $6

B. $7

C. $9

D. $12

E. $18

Question 11

Leoony makes a number pattern using these rules

- Choose four numbers
- After this, each number is the sum of the previous three numbers less the number before them.

Here is Leoony's pattern with three missing numbers labelled L, M and N.

1, L, 8, M, N, 19, 25

All of the numbers are whole numbers.

What number does N represent?

A. 2

B. 3

C. 10

D. 12

E. 14

Question 12

Malyn took up running aged 17 years old and ran competitively for 2 years before he had an injury which stopped him from running. He resumed when he was 37 years old. He then ran competitively until he was 45 years old. He then had a knee injury and stopped running for 1.5 years. Since then, Malyn has run regularly.

Assuming no more injuries, how old will Malyn be when the number of running years first exceeds the length of time he did not run?

A. 65 years old

B. 74 years and 6 months old

C. 73 years old

D. 72 years and 6 months old

E. 69 years old

Question 13

In a drawer there are five pairs of white socks, four pairs of blue socks, six pairs of red socks, two pairs of black socks and seven pairs of green socks.

In complete darkness, what is the minimum number of socks you need to take out of the drawer to be sure you have a green pair of socks?

A. 2

B. 18

C. 24

D. 34

E. 36

Question 14

A man bought a ring for $3,000 and sold it for $4,500. He then bought it back for $5,500 and resold it for $7,500. He then bought it again for $8,000 and sold it for $9,500.

What was his total profit?

A. $6,500

B. $3,500

C. $5,000

D. $5,500

E. $4,500

Question 15

What is twice three quarters of two fifths of 20?

A. 12

B. 6

C. 20

D. 8

E. 16

Question 16

There are four fields in an arrangement as shown below. The arrangement is drawn to scale. Corn is planted in each field in the same proportion. The second largest field contains 240 plants, each producing 100 pieces of corn.

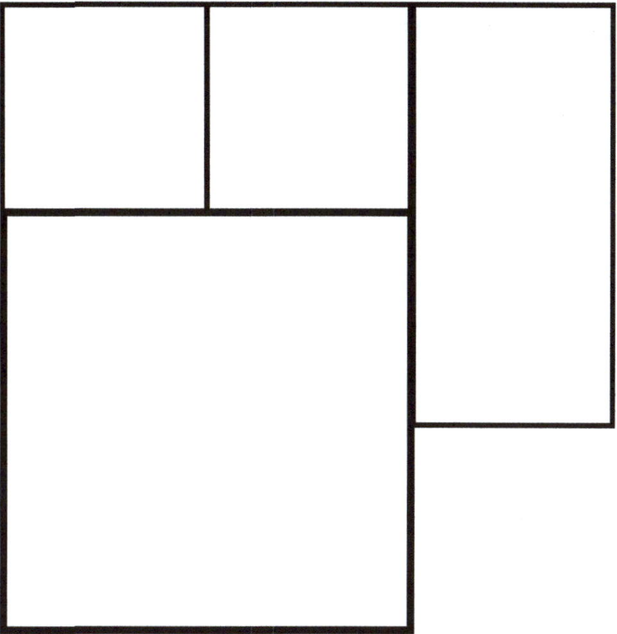

How many pieces of corn are produced in total by the four fields?

A. 240,000

B. 120,000

C. 96,000

D. 84,000

E. 48,000

Question 17

Four of these numbers have the same remainder when divided by 7.

54, 103, 131, 160, 215

Which of the numbers has a different remainder to the others?

A. 54

B. 103

C. 131

D. 160

E. 215

Question 18

The outside square has a perimeter of 80 cm, and the inside square has an area of 256 cm^2.

What is the perimeter of the small rectangle?

A. 48 cm

B. 24 cm

C. 18 cm

D. 34 cm

E. 28 cm

Question 19

What is the value of the missing number 🌰 in this pattern?

3, 3, 6, 🌰, 72, 360

A. 54

B. 18

C. 24

D. 60

E. 12

Question 20

Here are three identical bottles. The first is carrying 1,265 mL of water. The second is carrying 1.435 L of water. The third bottle is carrying juice.

After the contents of bottles 1 and 2 are poured into bottle 3, it is $^{2}/_{3}$ full. If there was 900 mL of juice in the third bottle, what is the volume of each bottle?

A. 4,800 mL

B. 5.2 L

C. 3,600 mL

D. 5,100 mL

E. 5.4 L

Image source: Water Bottle by Bernd Lakenbrink from NounProject.com

Question 21

In the prices below, each shape represents a missing digit.

$161.2○

$79.4△

What is the largest possible difference between the prices?

A. $82.81

B. $81.79

C. $81.71

D. $81.89

E. $81.81

Question 22

Leena has two different pairs of sandals, four different T-shirts and four different pairs of shorts.

Anna has three different pairs of sandals, three different T-shirts and four different pairs of shorts.

Who has a larger number of possible outfits, and by how many?

A. Anna has four more outfits than Leena

B. Leena has four more outfits than Anna

C. They both have the same number of outfits

D. Leena has two more outfits than Anna

E. Anna has two more outfits than Leena

Question 23

Donavi has a box of 54 toy animals. There are monkeys, lions, giraffes and gazelles. There are 8 monkeys in the box.

If he takes out an animal without looking, the probability it is a giraffe is $^1/_3$.

If $^2/_9$ of the animals in the box are lions, how many gazelles are in the box?

A. 38

B. 18

C. 36

D. 17

E. 16

Question 24

Here are some numerical playing cards

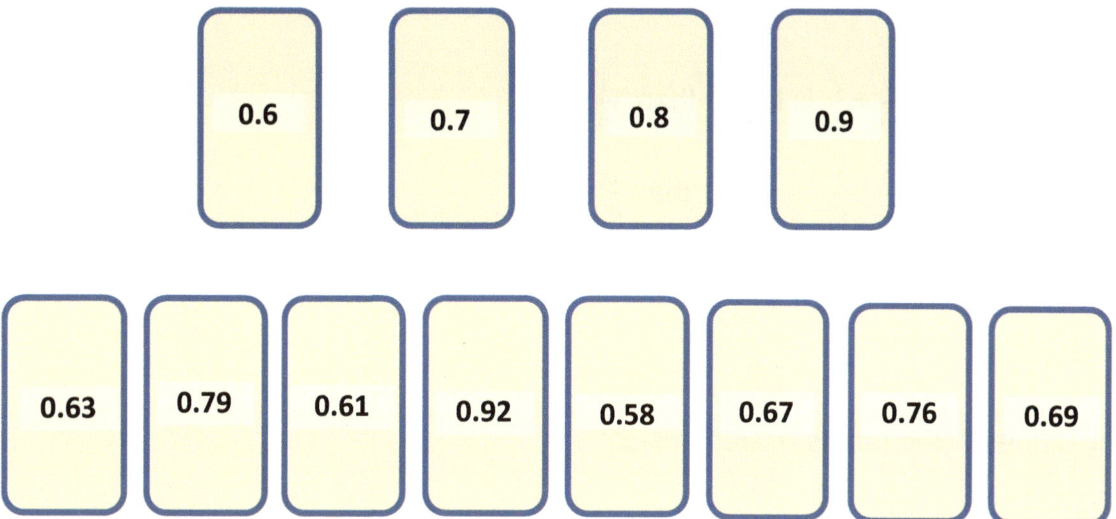

Sara arranges all the cards in a line, so that the numbers increase from left to right.

Which number will be the average of the two middle cards?

A. 0.695

B. 0.730

C. 0.750

D. 0.680

E. 0.780

Question 25

Look closely at the statements below:

Statement X $\frac{2}{3} + \frac{2}{3}$ is larger than $1\frac{1}{6}$

Statement Y $\frac{1}{5} - \frac{1}{15}$ is larger than $\frac{1}{8}$

Statement Z $\frac{7}{12} - \frac{1}{6}$ is smaller than $\frac{9}{24}$

Which of these statements is/are correct?

A. Statement Z only

B. Statement Y only

C. Statements Y and Z only

D. Statements X and Y only

E. Statements X and Z only

Question 26

Saiichi and Allie measure their heights using a vertical scale on the wall. The scale starts at 0 cm and goes up to 2 m. However, instead of the 0 being placed at ground level it was raised 15 cm above the ground.

Saiichi measures his height on the vertical scale, and it reads 146 cm.

Allie says, "*When I wear my 3 cm heels I am taller than you by 1 cm.*"

What is Allie's actual height?

A. 1.61 m

B. 1.59 m

C. 133 cm

D. 144 cm

E. 1.31 m

Source image: Measure by DinosoftLab from NounProject.com

Question 27

The time in Las Cruces is 17 hours behind the time in Sydney. The time in Suva is 2 hours ahead of the time in Sydney.

When it is 8 am on Wednesday in Suva what time is it in Las Cruces?

A. 5 pm on Tuesday
B. 3 am on Tuesday
C. 1 pm on Tuesday
D. 1 am on Wednesday
E. 7 pm on Tuesday

Question 28

Yunting, Shehla, Edward and Faisal and have some collectable cards. Yunting has 9 times as many cards as Faisal.

Shehla has $^{3}/_{5}$ as many as Edward

The ratio of cards Yunting has compared to Shehla is 6 : 1

If Yunting has 36 cards how many cards does Edward have?

A. 4
B. 20
C. 6
D. 12
E. 10

Question 29

In a survey, 100 children are asked their favourite colour. Dunith started to draw a graph but still has to finish the final three favourite colours.

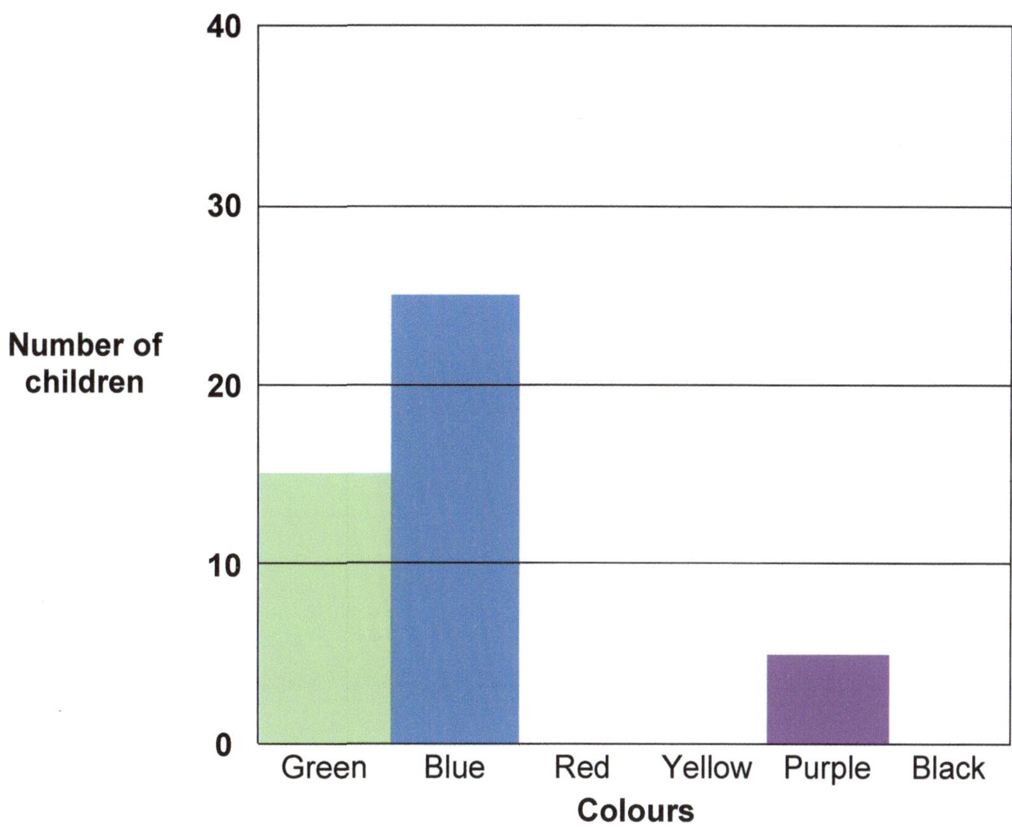

Dunith knows that the number of people who like black is half the number that like red. He also knows that the number of people who like yellow is one third of the number who like red.

How many people like red?

A. 38

B. 24

C. 36

D. 30

E. 42

Question 30

A cricket final sold 98,000 tickets over four days: Sunday, Monday, Tuesday and Wednesday.

- On Monday it sold two-thirds as many tickets as on Sunday.
- On Tuesday 22,000 tickets were sold.
- On Wednesday it sold two-thirds as many tickets as on Monday.

How many tickets were sold on Wednesday?

A. 76,000

B. 20,000

C. 36,000

D. 16,000

E. 18,000

Question 31

Here is a clock showing a time of 11 seconds to 20 minutes past 7. An alarm on the clock is set for 2 o'clock.

At exactly 7:20 what is the angle between the second hand and the hour hand?

A. 140°

B. 120°

C. 135°

D. 60°

E. 130°

Question 32

A number divided by 7, 5 and 3 leaves a remainder of 2.

A second number divided by 4, 5 and 9 leaves a remainder of 3.

What are the two possible numbers?

A. 73 and 23

B. 107 and 103

C. 212 and 363

D. 317 and 183

E. 107 and 147

Question 33

Look closely at the pattern below.

What symbol will be visible on the 45th tile from the left?

A.

B.

C.

D.

E.

Question 34

Five paper aeroplanes are thrown at the same time from sixth floor of a building. The height is 15 metres above the ground.

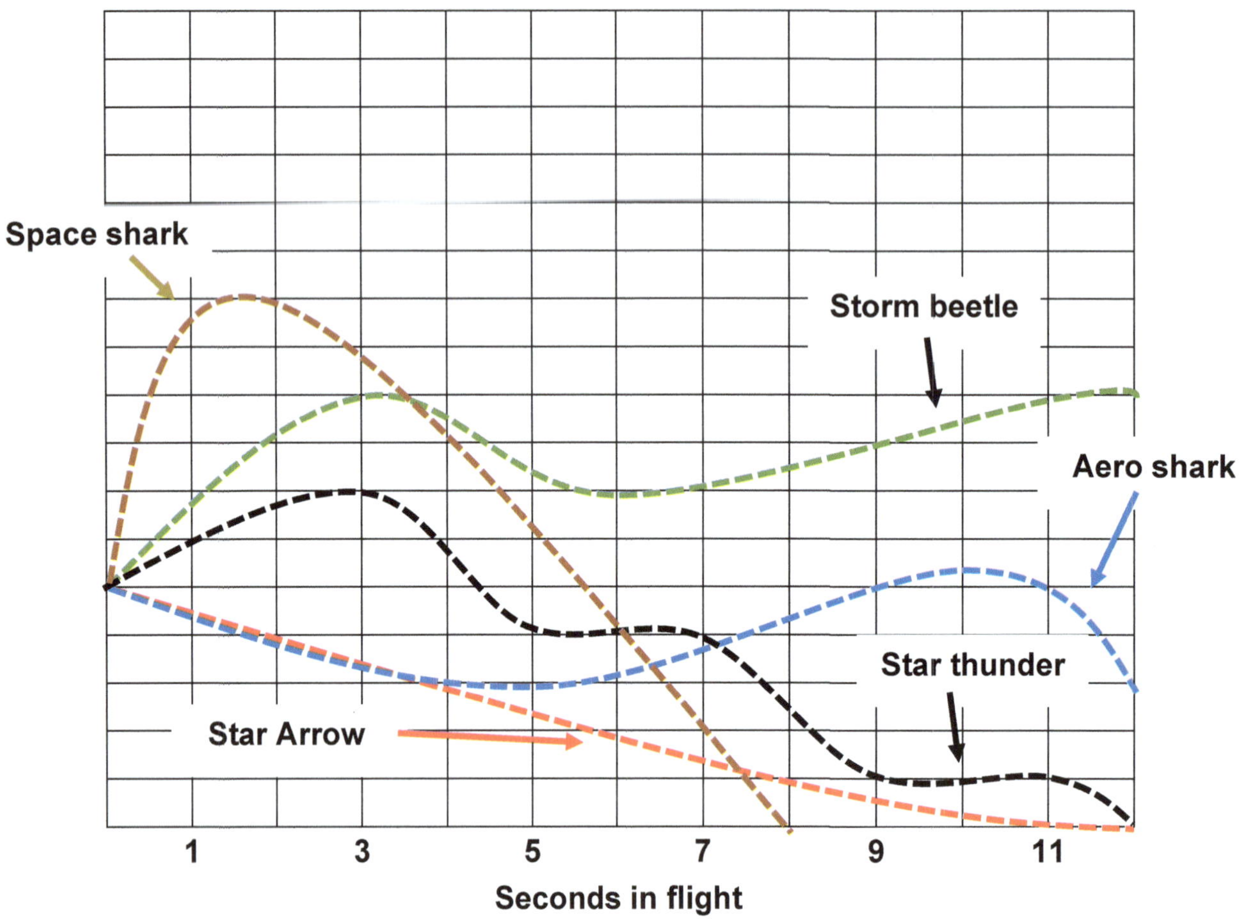

At 6 seconds after release which of the following is **true**?

A. Space Shark and Star Thunder are 9 metres below the Storm Beetle

B. Aero Shark is 9 metres off the ground and falling

C. Star Arrow is falling faster than all the other planes

D. Storm Beetle has flown furthest

E. Star Thunder is on its second period of level flight

Question 35

Six friends all live along the same long, straight road in this order:

Ross, Vanessa, Muneer, Ha, Tung, Vina

- Muneer lives 160 m from Tung but five times as far from Ross.
- Vina and Vanessa are equally far from Muneer.
- Vanessa is as far from Ross as she is from Tung.

If Ross walks to Vanessa's house, it takes him 3 minutes. Walking at the same pace, gets him to Muneer's house from his house in 5 minutes.

How far does Tung live from Vina?

A. 320 m

B. 160 m

C. 480 m

D. 800 m

E. 140 m

Question 36

A double semi-trailer holds 10,000 kg of boxed fruit. Three double semi-trailers hold the same number of kilograms as 75 logistics vans. Two logistics vans hold the same weight as five delivery cars.

What weight of boxed fruit can a single delivery car carry?

A. 300 kg

B. 160 kg

C. 400 kg

D. 80 kg

E. 180 kg

Question 37

Puppy and her friends like to catch bubbles.

- There is a one in ten chance that Alina will catch a bubble.
- There is a four in five that chance Puppy will catch a bubble.
- There is a one in three chance that Ilaria will catch a bubble.

Each of the girls has the opportunity to catch 30 bubbles.

Which of the following is **correct**?

A. Alina will catch 20 bubbles fewer than Puppy

B. Ilaria will catch three times as many bubbles as Alina

C. Puppy will catch two and a half times as many as Ilaria

D. Alina and Ilaria together catch fewer than Puppy

E. Ilaria and Puppy are more active than Alina

Source image: Kid Blowing Bubbles by Gan Khoon Lay from NounProject.com

Question 38

Junun is thinking of a whole number.

If he multiplies his number by 4 it is less than 42.
If he multiplies his number by 7 it is greater than 54

There is more than one number Junun could be thinking of.

What is the sum of all the numbers Junun could be thinking of?

A. 23

B. 24

C. 27

D. 34

E. 38

Question 39

If Stacey borrows money from the bank, she has to repay the amount she borrowed and also an additional amount. This amount is the cost of borrowing.

Stacey borrows four hundred and fifty dollars and for each ten dollars borrowed will repay an additional thirty cents.

How much does she repay in total?

A. $463.50

B. $450.30

C. $480.50

D. $458.30

E. $465.50

Question 40

Look closely at the arrangement and read the statements below.

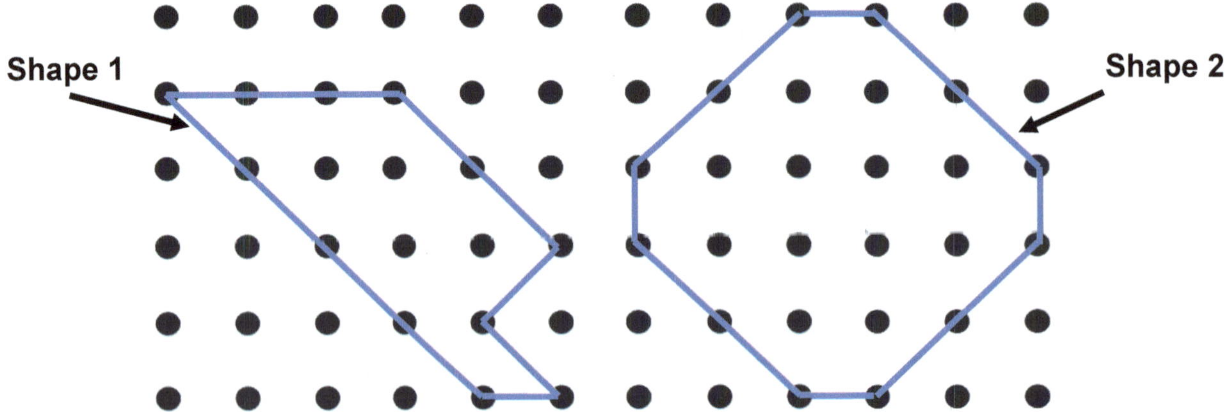

Statement 1 Shapes 1 and 2 have the same perimeter.

Statement 2 Shape 1 has a larger perimeter than shape 2.

Statement 3 Shape 1 has a larger area than shape 2.

Statement 4 Shapes 1 and 2 have the same area.

Statement 5 Shape 2 has a larger area than shape 1

Statement 6 Shape 2 has a larger perimeter than shape 1.

Which of the following statements is/are correct?

A. Statement 1 and 5 only

B. Statements 1 only

C. Statements 1 and 4 only

D. Statements 5 and 6 only

E. Statement 5 only

Image source: Grid by Viktor Vorobyev from NounProject.com

Question 41

The sum of the numbers in each row, column and diagonal of this square, are the same. No number is repeated, and all the digits are from 1 to 9.

6	Y	2X
	5	3
		X

What number should be at Y?

A. 5
B. 2
C. 3
D. 1
E. 4

Question 42

The graph below shows the percentage of different gases in air and in salt water.

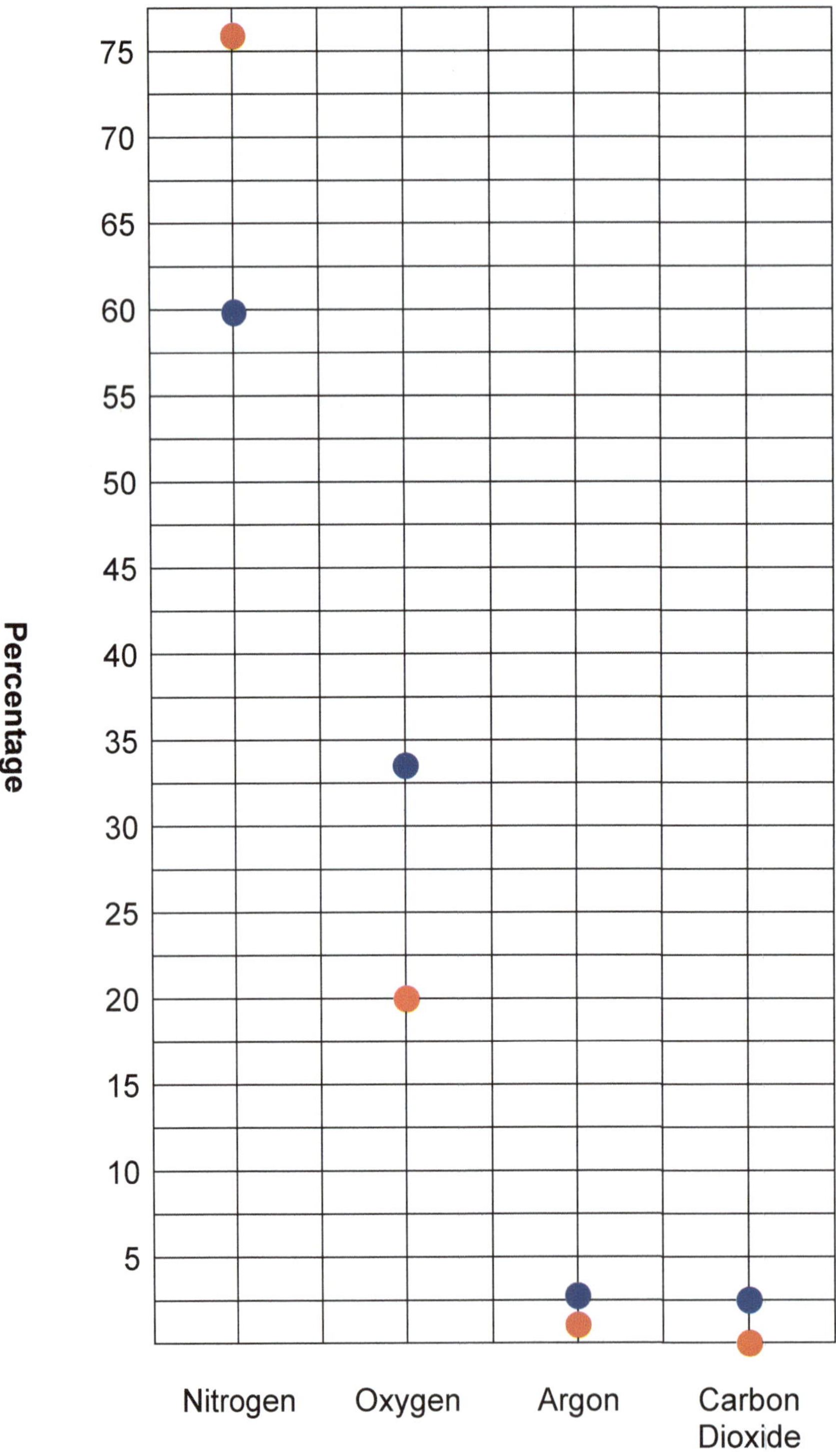

Key

- Percentage of gas in salt water
- Percentage of gas in air

Statement 1 Nitrogen has twice the percentage in air than oxygen has in water

Statement 2 Carbon dioxide is 2.5 times more present in salt water than in air

Statement 3 Nitrogen is the only gas with a lower percentage in salt water than air

Statement 4 Carbon dioxide is less present in air than salt water

Which of the following is **true**?

A. Statement 2 and Statement 4 only

B. Statement 3 and Statement 4 only

C. Statement 2 only

D. Statements 2, 3 and 4 only

E. Statement 3 only

Question 43

Mandy can buy 1 bread roll for 60 cents, 2 for $1.10, 6 for $2.80.

What is the largest number of bread rolls Mandy can buy for $16?

A. 36 rolls
B. 34 rolls
C. 33 rolls
D. 32 rolls
E. 31 rolls

Question 44

Which of these numbers is closest to 1?

A. 1.0090
B. 0.9920
C. 1.0100
D. 0.0999
E. 1.0081

Question 45

Four racing car drivers start from the indicated start/finish spot. It takes one of the cars 2 minutes to complete the 4-kilometre circuit. Another one takes 1 minute and 45 seconds. A third takes 1 minute and the last one takes 1 minute and 30 seconds.

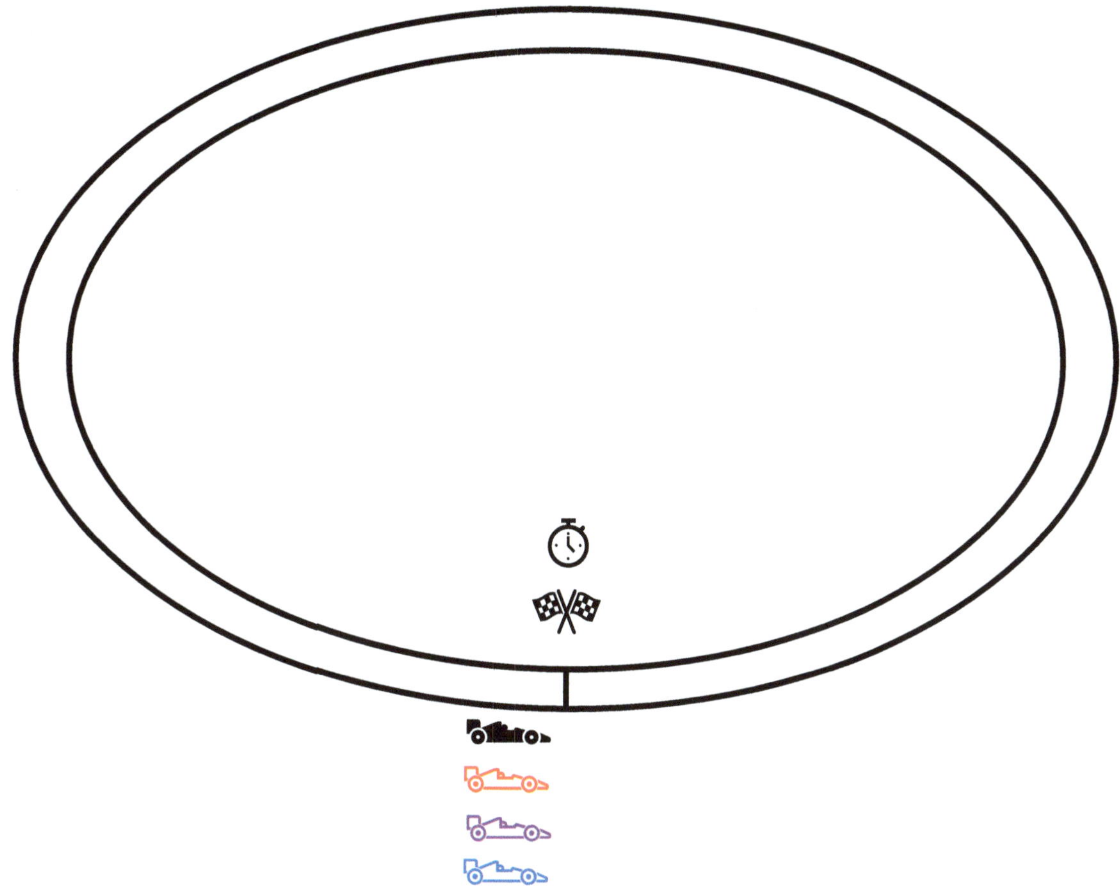

How long after they commence will it take for the cars to pass the starting line together?

A. 6 minutes

B. 12 minutes

C. 14 minutes

D. 24 minutes

E. 42 minutes

Question 46

When this drink bottle is one quarter full, the bottle and the water inside together weigh 175 grams.

When this drink bottle is three-quarters full, the water inside and the bottle together weigh 325 grams.

What is the weight of the bottle and the drink inside together when the bottle is four-fifths full?

A. 360 grams

B. 500 grams

C. 420 grams

D. 350 grams

E. 340 grams

Image source: Drinking Bottle by Jae Deasigner from NounProject.com

Question 47

This shape, made of 48 identical cubes was submerged fully in water.

How many cube faces did not get wet?

A. 72

B. 144

C. 170

D. 196

E. 154

Question 48

Jessy catches the third train of the day to There from Here and returns to Here from There on the third train back.

From Here to There		From There to Here	
Leaves at 8:30 am	Arrives at 10:45 am	Leaves at 09:15 am	Arrives at 11:45 am
Leaves at 11:30 am	Arrives at 01:45 pm	Leaves at 12:15 pm	Arrives at 02:45 pm
Leaves at 02:30 pm	Arrives at 04:45 pm	Leaves at 03:45 pm	Arrives at 06:15 pm
Leaves at 05:30 pm	Arrives at 07:45 pm	Leaves at 06:15 pm	Arrives at 08:45 pm
Leaves at 08:30 pm	Arrives at 10:45 pm	Leaves at 09:45 pm	Arrives at 12:15 am

How long is she away from Here?

A. 21 hours and 15 minutes

B. 24 hours and 15 minutes

C. 19 hours exactly

D. 3 hours and 45 minutes

E. 9 hours and 45 minutes

Question 49

Here are three measuring cups:

When the bottom measuring cup is two thirds full it can fill two and a half of the top measuring cup.

When the top measuring cup is full how much of the bottom measuring cup can it fill?

A. Five fourths

B. Three fifths

C. Nine twentieths

D. Four fifteenths

E. One third

Source image: Measuring Cups by Chaowalit Koetchuea from NounProject.com

Question 50

Here is a shape made of black and white parts.

The bottom right hand black square is 3 cm × 3 cm.

What area in this shape is shaded?

A. 221 cm^2

B. 360 cm^2

C. 316 cm^2

D. 283 cm^2

E. 259 cm^2

Answers

Answers

Summary of Answers

1	D	11	D	21	D	31	A	41	D
2	E	12	C	22	A	32	C	42	B
3	C	13	E	23	E	33	E	43	C
4	E	14	C	24	A	34	A	44	B
5	C	15	A	25	D	35	B	45	E
6	D	16	C	26	B	36	B	46	E
7	B	17	D	27	C	37	D	47	C
8	C	18	B	28	E	38	C	48	A
9	A	19	B	29	D	39	A	49	D
10	B	20	E	30	D	40	A	50	E

A = 9, 15, 22, 24, 31, 34, 39, 40, 48
B = 7, 10, 18, 19, 26, 35, 36, 42, 44
C = 3, 5, 8, 12, 14, 27, 32, 38, 43, 47
D = 1, 6, 11, 21, 25, 29, 30, 37, 49
E = 2, 4, 13, 20, 23, 28, 33, 41, 45, 46, 50

Answers

Fully worked solutions

Question 1

D.

1/6 of 168 is 28. So, they get 28 decisions correct and 140 incorrect.

Question 2

E.

1 of the 18 survivors, 1 of the survivors, 9 = 1 + 8, 0.1 = 18 ÷ 180 the number of passengers, 12 = 1 × 6 × 2 = (the sum of the digits of the number who perished).

Question 3

C.

Sum of the digits of prime numbers between 10 and 100:
11: 2 (prime)
13: 4 (square)
17: 8 (cube)
19: 10
23: 5 (prime)
29: 11 (prime)
31: 4 (square)
37: 10
41: 5 (prime)
43: 7 (prime)
47: 11 (prime)
53: 8 (cube)
59: 14
61: 7 (prime)
67: 13 (prime)
71: 8 (cube)
73: 10
79: 16 (square)
83: 11 (prime)
89: 17 (prime)
97: 16 (square)

There are 10 that have digits that add to a prime number and 4 that have digits that add to a square. The difference is 6.

Question 4

E.

A following the pattern can give this: 96 from (8 × 11) + 8

B following the pattern can give this: 40 from 2 + 5 + (5) = 12, 3 + 6 + (12) = 21, 8 + 11 + (21) = 40

C following the pattern can give this: 52 from 1 + (4 × 1) = 5, 2 + (5 × 2) = 12, 3 + (6 × 3) = 21, 8 + (11 × 4) = 52

D following the pattern gives this: 92 from (1 × 4) + 1 = 5, (2 × 5) + 2 = 12, (3 × 6) + 3 = 21, (8 × 11) + 4 = 92

E 42 cannot be derived following rules.

Question 5

C.

2.10.2 = 14 = 2 pm, 1 + 9 + 3 = 13 = 1 pm, so 9 + 4 + 9 = 22 = 10 pm

Question 6

D.

Midnight reads as 12*
1 am reads as 3
2 am reads as 6
3 am reads as 9
4 am reads as 12
5 am reads as 3
6 am reads as 6*
7 am reads as 9
8 am reads as 12
9 am reads as 3
10 am reads as 6
11 am reads as 9
NOON reads as 12*
1 pm reads as 3
2 pm reads as 6
3 pm reads as 9
4 pm reads as 12
5 pm reads as 3
6 pm reads as 6*
7 pm reads as 9
8 pm reads as 12
9 pm reads as 3
10 pm reads as 6
11 pm reads as 9
Midnight reads as 12* (this is included as this completes the 24 hours)

Question 7

B.

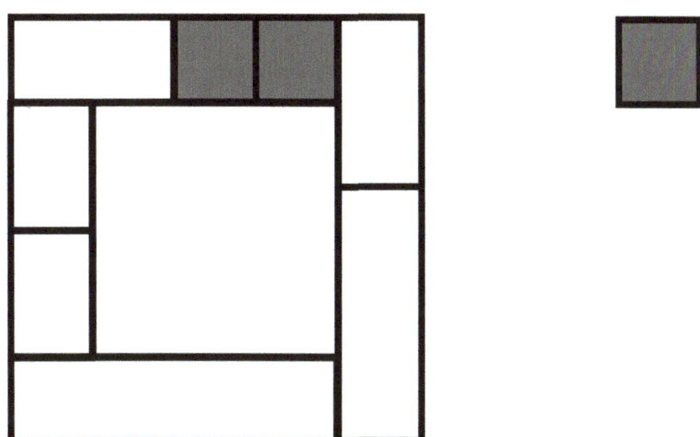

The shape is 5 × 5 of the small square, hence 2/25 is shaded.

Question 8

C.

5 × 365 (Sept 9th 1961 – Sept 9th 1966) + [30 × 2 (November and the rest of September and early days in January)] + [31 × 2 (October and December)] + 1 (1 leap year, 1964) + 4 days (the difference between 9th and 13th) = 1952

Question 9

A.

Lester's number is a multiple of 7.
Brintu's number is an even number which is a multiple of 9.
Kanav's number is an odd number between 71 and 90

What is the difference between the largest possible value of Kanav's number and the largest difference between Lester and Brintu's numbers?

Lester's number is 42, Brintu's number is 90 and Kanav's number is 89. The difference between Brintu and Lester's numbers is 48.

The difference between this and 89 is 41.

Question 10

B.

Coyne had $50.

He gave half of his money to Albert. This leaves Coyne with $25. If Rajeev got $1.50 then Floyd got $6.00. This is a third of $18.00 which means after he gave money to Misty, he had $18. He therefore gave Misty $7.

Question 11

D.

$L + 8 + M - 1 = N$ – equation 1

$8 + M + N - L = 19$ – equation 2

$M + N + 19 - 8 = 25$. – equation 3 - From this we know that $M + N = 14$ – equation 4

Hence, from equation 2, $L = 3$

From equation 1, $L + 8 + M - 1 = N$, so $3 + 8 + M - 1 = N$

So, $M + 10 = N$ – equation 5

We also know that $M = 14 - N$ (from equation 4)

So, $14 - N + 10 = N$ (substituting 4 into 5)

Hence, $24 = 2N$ so, $N = 12$ and $M = 2$

The pattern is: 1, 3, 8, 2, 12, 19, 25

Question 12

C.

Not running: $17 + (37 - 19) + 1.5 = 17 + 18 + 1.5 = 36.5$ years

Hence running would be $36.5 + 36.5 = 73$ years old

Question 13

E.

To be assured of getting two green socks then it must be assumed that all of the other sock pairs have been drawn first. There are five pairs of white socks, four pairs of blue socks, six pairs of red socks, two pairs of black socks: totalling 17 pairs or 34 socks. Two more socks need to be drawn out to be assured of a pair of green socks — hence 36 socks.

Question 14

C.

Initial profit is $4,500 − $3,000 = $1,500. He then makes $2,000 ($7,500 − $5,500) and $1,500 ($9,000 − $7,500).

The total profit is therefore: $1,500 + $2,000 + $1,500 = $5,000

Question 15

A.

Twice three quarters of two fifths of 20:

8 is two fifths of 20. Three quarters of this is 6. Twice 6 is 12.

Question 16

C.

In this arrangement, the second largest field is equal in size to the two smallest fields and is half as large as the largest field. This field can produce 240 × 100 pieces of corn – 24,000 pieces. This would be the same as the sum of the number of corn pieces produced by the smallest fields and would be half that produced by the largest field (48,000). Accordingly, the total number of corn pieces produced would be 24,000 (2 smallest fields) + 24,000 (second largest field) + 48,000 (largest field = 96,000 pieces.

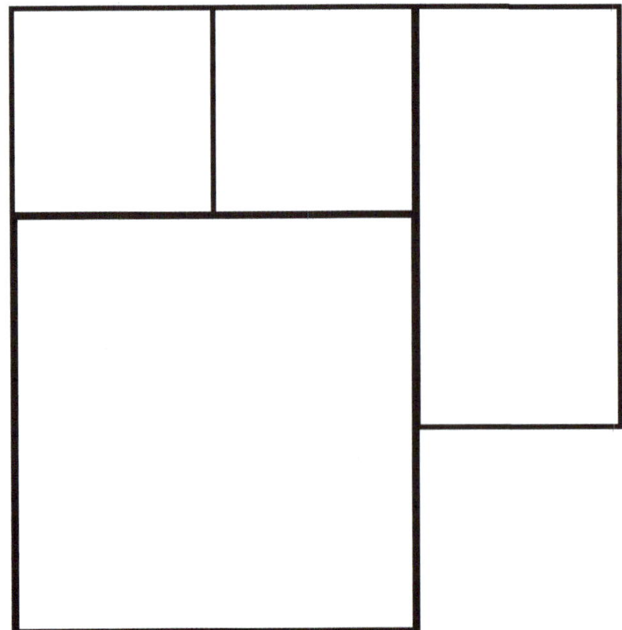

Question 17

D.

Four of these numbers have the same remainder when divided by 7.

54, 103, 131, 160, 215

Each of these numbers when divided by 7 have a remainder of 5, except 160, which when divided by 7 has a remainder of 6.

Question 18

B.

Each of the sides of the large square must be 20 cm long. Hence half of that is 10cm. So, the rectangle is 10 cm long. The sides of the small square must be 16 cm each, as 16 × 16 = 256.

This means that the width of the blue strips must be 2 cm.

Hence the perimeter of the rectangle must be 10 cm + 2 cm + 10 cm + 2 cm = 24 cm.

Question 19

B.

The second number is the first number multiplied by 1, the third number is the second number multiplied by 2, the fourth number (hidden) is the third number multiplied by 3, the fifth number is the fourth number multiplied by 4 and the sixth number is the fifth number multiplied by 5.

The pattern is: 3, 3, 6, 18, 72, 360

Question 20

E.

1,265 + 1,435 + 900 = 3.6 L

3.6 L is $^{2}/_{3}$ full hence full is 5.4 litres

Question 21

D.

The largest difference will arise when the bigger number is as high as possible and the lower number is as small as possible. This means that the circle should be a 9 and the triangle a 0. The largest difference must therefore end with a 9 (9 – 0).

Question 22

A.

Leena's options

Sandal 1
T-shirt 1, Shorts 1, 2, 3 or 4 (4 combinations)
T-shirt 2, Shorts 1, 2, 3 or 4 (4 combinations)
T-shirt 3, Shorts 1, 2, 3 or 4 (4 combinations)
T-shirt 4, Shorts 1, 2, 3 or 4 (4 combinations)

Sandal 2
T-shirt 1, Shorts 1, 2, 3 or 4 (4 combinations)
T-shirt 2, Shorts 1, 2, 3 or 4 (4 combinations)
T-shirt 3, Shorts 1, 2, 3 or 4 (4 combinations)
T-shirt 4, Shorts 1, 2, 3 or 4 (4 combinations)

Total combinations: 32

Anna's options

Sandal 1
T-shirt 1, Shorts 1, 2, 3 or 4 (4 combinations)
T-shirt 2, Shorts 1, 2, 3 or 4 (4 combinations)
T-shirt 3, Shorts 1, 2, 3 or 4 (4 combinations)

Sandal 2
T-shirt 1, Shorts 1, 2, 3 or 4 (4 combinations)
T-shirt 2, Shorts 1, 2, 3 or 4 (4 combinations)
T-shirt 3, Shorts 1, 2, 3 or 4 (4 combinations)

<u>Sandal 3</u>
T-shirt 1, Shorts 1, 2, 3 or 4 (4 combinations)
T-shirt 2, Shorts 1, 2, 3 or 4 (4 combinations)
T-shirt 3, Shorts 1, 2, 3 or 4 (4 combinations)

Total combinations: 36

Hence A is correct.

Question 23

E.

There 54 animals 8 of which are monkeys. This leaves 46 animals. If $^1/_3$ of the total animals are giraffes, then this means 18 animals are giraffes. $^2/_9$ of the animals are lions, which equates to 12 lions. This means that 8 + 18 + 12 = 38 animals are accounted for. There are 54 − 38 = 16 gazelles in the box.

Question 24

A.

The numbers in order are:

0.58, 0.6, 0.61, 0.63, 0.67, **<u>0.69, 0.7</u>**, 0.76, 0.79, 0.8, 0.9, 0.92

The middle two numbers (the sixth and seventh) are highlighted.

The average of 0.69 and 0.70 = 0.695.

Question 25

D.

Statement X $\frac{2}{3}+\frac{2}{3}$ is $\frac{4}{3}$ or $1\frac{2}{6}$ and IS larger than $1\frac{1}{6}$ so **X is correct**

Statement Y $\frac{1}{5}-\frac{1}{15}$ is $\frac{2}{15}$ and is larger than $\frac{1}{8}$ so **Y is also correct**

Statement Z

$\frac{7}{12}-\frac{1}{6}$ is $\frac{5}{12}$ which is $\frac{10}{24}$ and is larger NOT smaller than $\frac{9}{24}$ **so Z is incorrect**

Question 26

B.

1.59 m. A reading of 146 cm is actually a height of 146 + 15 = 161 cm as the zero on the vertical scale is 15 centimetres above the ground. This means that Saiichi is 161 cm tall. Allie is 2 centimetres shorter than Saiichi because if she is raised 3 cm she is 162 cm (1 cm taller than Saiichi). Consequently, her height must be 159 cm or 1.59 m.

Question 27

C.

The difference between Suva and Las Cruces must be Suva, being 19 hours ahead. Consequently, the time in Las Cruces as 8 am Suva time is 19 hours behind – which is 1 pm the day before.

Question 28

E.

Yunting has 36 cards which is 9 times as many as Faisal. Faisal has 4 cards. Since the ratio of Yunting's cards to Shehla's cards is 6 : 1 then Shehla has 6 cards. If 6 is $^{3}/_{5}$ of Edward's cards, then Edward has 10 cards. There are 56 cards in total.

Question 29

D.

15 Green

Blue 25

10 Yellow
Black 15
Red 30
Purple 5

$x + x/2 + x/3 = 55$

Hence $15/6x = 55$ or $11/6x = 55$. $1/6x = 55/11 = 5$. Hence $x = 30$

Question 30

D.

98,000 tickets went on sale and 22,000 were sold on Tuesday. This means 76,000 were sold on the other three days.

Let the number of tickets sold on Sunday be Y.

$^2/_3Y$ is sold on Monday, $^2/_3 \times {}^2/_3Y$ is sold on Wednesday.

The sum of these is: $Y + {}^2/_3Y + ({}^2/_3 \times {}^2/_3Y)$

$= Y + {}^2/_3Y + {}^4/_9Y$

$= Y + {}^6/_9Y + {}^4/_9Y$

$= Y + {}^{10}/_9Y = {}^{19}/_9Y$

$76{,}000 = {}^{19}/_9Y$, so $(9 \times 76{,}000)/19 = Y$

Hence Y = 36,000.

So, 24,000 were sold on Monday and 16,000 on Wednesday.

Question 31

A.

The angle between each of the clock numbers is 30°. Counter-clockwise from 12 to 8 is 120°. The hour hand shall have moved a third of the distance between the 7 and 8 or an angle of 10°. Therefore, an additional 20° is required to get to the 8 on the clockface. This means that the overall angle will be 120° + 20° = 140 degrees.

Question 32

C.

Question 33

E.

Symbol	Where found (numbered squares from the left)
	Squares 1, 3, 6, 10, 15, 21, 28, 36, 45, 55
	Squares 2, 6 (hidden), 14, 30, 62
	Squares: 1 (hidden), 5, 9, 13, 17, 21 (hidden), 25, 29, 33 (hidden), 37, 41, **45** (hidden), 49
	Squares 4, 8, 12, 16, 20, 24, 28, 32, 36 (hidden), 40, 44 (may be hidden), 48
	Squares 7, 11, 18, 22, 29, 33, 40, 44 (may be hidden), 51

Empty squares: 19, 23, 26, 27, 31, 34, 35, 38, 39, 42, 46, 47 and 50

Question 34

A.

Five paper aeroplanes are thrown at the same time from sixth floor of a building. The height is 15 metres above the ground.

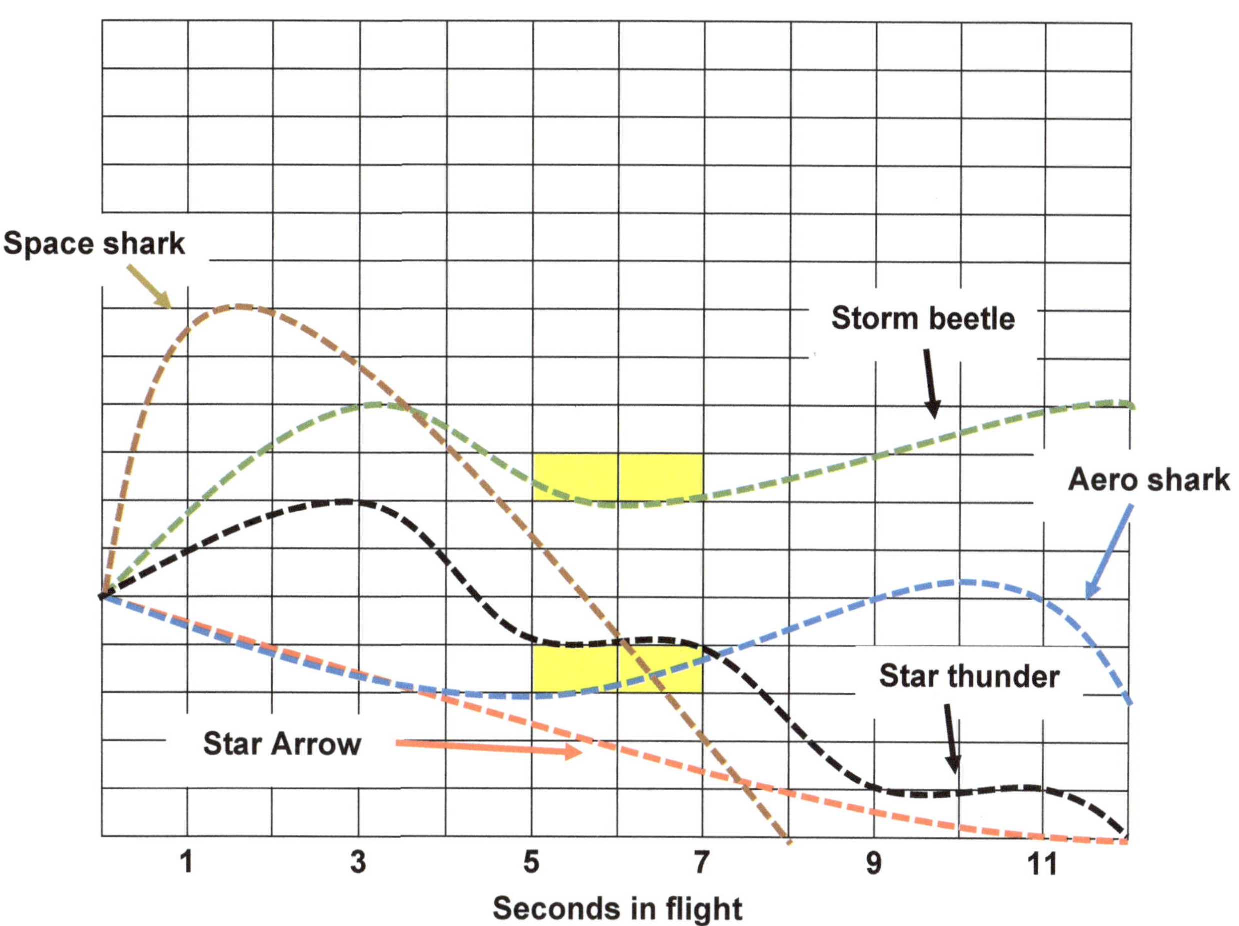

At 6 seconds after release A is true: as Space Shark and Star Thunder are 9 metres below the Storm Beetle. This is true as highlighted

B. is incorrect as Aero Shark is 9 metres off the ground and rising

C. is incorrect as Space Shark is faster than all the other planes

D. Is incorrect as it is not possible to tell which plane has flown furthest. Only which may be in flight for the longest time (Storm Beetle)

E. Is incorrect as Star Thunder is on its first period of level flight (not second period)

Question 35

B.

Muneer lives 160 m from Tung but five times as far from Ross. This means that the distance between Muneer and Tung is 800 m.

Ross ←→ Vanessa ←→ Muneer ←→ Ha ←→ Tung ←→ Vina

←--------- 800 m-----------→←---------160 m-----→

If Ross walks to Vanessa's house it takes him 3 minutes. Walking at the same pace gets him to Muneer's house in 5 minutes.

This means that Vanessa is 480m ($^3/_5$ × 800) from Ross and 320m ($^2/_5$ × 800) from Muneer:

Ross ←→ (480 m) Vanessa ←→ (320 m) Muneer ←→ Ha ←→ Tung ←→ Vina

Vina and Vanessa are equally far from Muneer.

Ross ←→ (480 m) Vanessa ←→ (320 m) Muneer ←→ Ha ←→ Tung ←→ Vina
←---------160 m-----→
←----------- 320 m ------------→

Therefore, Tung must live 160 m from Vina.

Vanessa is as far from Ross as she is from Tung. (This is not required)

Question 36

B.

10,000 × 3 = 30,000 kg

30,000 ÷ 75 = 400 kg

2 × 400 = 800 kg

800 ÷ 5 = 160 kg

Question 37

D.

Alina will catch an average of 3 of 30 bubbles, Puppy will catch 24 of her 30 and Ilaria will catch 10 of her 30.

Question 38

C.

The following numbers satisfy the first condition: 1, 2, 3, 4, 5, 6, 7, **8, 9 and 10.**

The following numbers satisfy the second condition: **8, 9, 10,** 11, 12, 13....etc

The possible numbers that satisfy BOTH conditions are: 8, 9, 10

Question 39

A.

$450 ÷ 10 = $45.

45 × $0.30 = 1,350 cents = $13.50. The total amount is therefore $450 + $13.50 = $463.50

Question 40

A.

Question 41

D.

Here is the completed square:

6	1	8
7	5	3
2	9	4

X cannot be either 3 or 5 as these numbers have been used. Moreover, 5 doubled is 10 – which is disallowed.

X cannot be 1 as this would make 2X = 2 and the right-hand column would add to 6 (2 + 3 + 1) – different to the diagonal (adding to 12 in this case)

X cannot be 2 as this would make the diagonal 13 and the right hand column 4 + 3 + 2 = 9 (unequal)

X must be 4.

This means that all rows, columns and diagonals add to 15. Hence Y is 1.

Question 42

B.

Question 43

C.

1 roll: 60 cents

2 rolls: $1.10 = 55 cents each

6 rolls: $2.80 = 46.7 cents each

5 × $2.80 = $14 = 30 rolls

1 × $1.10 = $15.10 = 32 rolls

1 × $0.60 = $15.70 = 33 rolls (Change 30 cents)

Please note: hypothetically, $16 ÷ 46.7 cents = 34.3, implying a possibility of 34 rolls being purchased for $16. However, since the rolls can only be bought in discrete amounts, this answer must be wrong.

Question 44

B.

A is 90 ten thousandths too high.

B is 80 ten thousandths too low 0.9920.

C is 100 ten thousandths too high.

D is 0.9001 too low.

E is 81 ten thousandths too high.

Accordingly, B is closest to 1.

Question 45

E.

Times back to start/finish line:

	Times back to the start/finish line														
C1	2	4	**6**	8	10	12	14	16	18	20	22	24	26	…	42
C2	1.45	3.30	5.15	**7**	8.45	10.30	12.15	14	15.45	17.30	19.15	21	22.45	…	42
C3	1	2	3	4	5	6	7	8	9	10	11	12	13	…	42
C4	1.30	3	4.30	6	7.30	9	10.30	12	13.30	15	16.30	18	19.30	…	42

The lowest common multiple of 6 and 7 is 42 so this should be the next time the cars are altogether at the starting line.

Question 46

E.

When this drink bottle is one quarter full, the bottle and the water inside together weigh 175 grams and when this drink bottle is three-quarters full, the water inside and the bottle, together 325 weigh grams. The difference of 150 grams must be the weight of the water (in a half full bottle). This means that a full bottle can hold 300 grams of water.

A quarter of 300 is 75 grams, so the bottle must weigh 100 grams.

Hence the weight of the bottle four fifths full must be 100g + $^4/_5 \times 300$ = 340 grams.

Question 47

C.

48 blocks have 288 faces. Touching faces will not get wet.

Back rows:
Top blocks touching: 8
Top blocks on 2nd row: 10
2nd row block touching each other: 22
2nd row resting on 8 blocks: 16
These 8 blocks side by side: 14
2nd row back touch middle row: 20

Middle row blocks touching each other: 20
Middle bottom row touching 8 blocks below: 16
Bottom middle blocks touching back 8 blocks: 16
Bottom middle row blocks touching each other: 14

Front row touching middle row: 8
Front blocks touching each other: 6

Total touching faces: 170

Question 48

A.

From Here to There		From There to Here	
Leaves at 8:30 am	Arrives at 10:45 am	Leaves at 09:15 am	Arrives at 11:45 am
Leaves at 11:30 am	Arrives at 01:45 pm	Leaves at 12:15 pm	Arrives at 02:45 pm
Leaves at 02:30 pm	Arrives at 04:45 pm	Leaves at 03:45 pm	Arrives at 06:15 pm
Leaves at 05:30 pm	Arrives at 07:45 pm	Leaves at 06:15 pm	Arrives at 08:45 pm
Leaves at 08:30 pm	Arrives at 10:45 pm	Leaves at 09:45 pm	Arrives at 12:15 am

2:30 pm one day to 11:45 am the next day is 21 hours and 15 minutes in total.

Question 49

D.

Two thirds of the bottom cup equals 2.5 top cups.

$2/3x = 5/2\ y$

$1/3x = 5/4y$

$1/3 \times 4/5 = 4/15$

Question 50

E.

The shape is 20 cm × 20 cm = 400 sq cm.

9 + (3 × 8) + (3 × 5) + 19 (10 + 9) + 23 (12 + 11) + [(2 × 16)] + (2 × 13) + 60 + (17 × 3)
= 9 + 24 + 15 +19 + 23 + 32 + 26 + 60 + 51
= 9 + 39 + 42 + 58 + 111
= 259 cm^2.

Answers

Mathematical Reasoning

FOR SELECTIVE SCHOOL TESTS,
OPPORTUNITY CLASS TEST
AND PROBLEM SOLVING

Use pencil when filling out this sheet

Fill in the circle correctly				
●	(D)	(O)	(D)	(C)

If you make a mistake neatly cross it out and circle the correct response				
⊗	●	(C)	(D)	(E)

MULTIPLE CHOICE ANSWER SHEET

1	(A)	(B)	(C)	(D)	(E)	26	(A)	(B)	(C)	(D)	(E)
2	(A)	(B)	(C)	(D)	(E)	27	(A)	(B)	(C)	(D)	(E)
3	(A)	(B)	(C)	(D)	(E)	28	(A)	(B)	(C)	(D)	(E)
4	(A)	(B)	(C)	(D)	(E)	29	(A)	(B)	(C)	(D)	(E)
5	(A)	(B)	(C)	(D)	(E)	30	(A)	(B)	(C)	(D)	(E)
6	(A)	(B)	(C)	(D)	(E)	31	(A)	(B)	(C)	(D)	(E)
7	(A)	(B)	(C)	(D)	(E)	32	(A)	(B)	(C)	(D)	(E)
8	(A)	(B)	(C)	(D)	(E)	33	(A)	(B)	(C)	(D)	(E)
9	(A)	(B)	(C)	(D)	(E)	34	(A)	(B)	(C)	(D)	(E)
10	(A)	(B)	(C)	(D)	(E)	35	(A)	(B)	(C)	(D)	(E)
11	(A)	(B)	(C)	(D)	(E)	36	(A)	(B)	(C)	(D)	(E)
12	(A)	(B)	(C)	(D)	(E)	37	(A)	(B)	(C)	(D)	(E)
13	(A)	(B)	(C)	(D)	(E)	38	(A)	(B)	(C)	(D)	(E)
14	(A)	(B)	(C)	(D)	(E)	39	(A)	(B)	(C)	(D)	(E)
15	(A)	(B)	(C)	(D)	(E)	40	(A)	(B)	(C)	(D)	(E)
16	(A)	(B)	(C)	(D)	(E)	41	(A)	(B)	(C)	(D)	(E)
17	(A)	(B)	(C)	(D)	(E)	42	(A)	(B)	(C)	(D)	(E)
18	(A)	(B)	(C)	(D)	(E)	43	(A)	(B)	(C)	(D)	(E)
19	(A)	(B)	(C)	(D)	(E)	44	(A)	(B)	(C)	(D)	(E)
20	(A)	(B)	(C)	(D)	(E)	45	(A)	(B)	(C)	(D)	(E)
21	(A)	(B)	(C)	(D)	(E)	46	(A)	(B)	(C)	(D)	(E)
22	(A)	(B)	(C)	(D)	(E)	47	(A)	(B)	(C)	(D)	(E)
23	(A)	(B)	(C)	(D)	(E)	48	(A)	(B)	(C)	(D)	(E)
24	(A)	(B)	(C)	(D)	(E)	49	(A)	(B)	(C)	(D)	(E)
25	(A)	(B)	(C)	(D)	(E)	50	(A)	(B)	(C)	(D)	(E)

Mathematical Reasoning

FOR SELECTIVE SCHOOL TESTS, OPPORTUNITY CLASS TEST AND PROBLEM SOLVING

Use pencil when filling out this sheet

Fill in the circle correctly				
●	Ⓑ	Ⓒ	Ⓓ	Ⓔ

If you make a mistake neatly cross it out and circle the correct response				
⊗	●	Ⓒ	Ⓓ	Ⓔ

MULTIPLE CHOICE ANSWER SHEET

1	Ⓐ	Ⓑ	Ⓒ	Ⓓ	Ⓔ	26	Ⓐ	Ⓑ	Ⓒ	Ⓓ	Ⓔ
2	Ⓐ	Ⓑ	Ⓒ	Ⓓ	Ⓔ	27	Ⓐ	Ⓑ	Ⓒ	Ⓓ	Ⓔ
3	Ⓐ	Ⓑ	Ⓒ	Ⓓ	Ⓔ	28	Ⓐ	Ⓑ	Ⓒ	Ⓓ	Ⓔ
4	Ⓐ	Ⓑ	Ⓒ	Ⓓ	Ⓔ	29	Ⓐ	Ⓑ	Ⓒ	Ⓓ	Ⓔ
5	Ⓐ	Ⓑ	Ⓒ	Ⓓ	Ⓔ	30	Ⓐ	Ⓑ	Ⓒ	Ⓓ	Ⓔ
6	Ⓐ	Ⓑ	Ⓒ	Ⓓ	Ⓔ	31	Ⓐ	Ⓑ	Ⓒ	Ⓓ	Ⓔ
7	Ⓐ	Ⓑ	Ⓒ	Ⓓ	Ⓔ	32	Ⓐ	Ⓑ	Ⓒ	Ⓓ	Ⓔ
8	Ⓐ	Ⓑ	Ⓒ	Ⓓ	Ⓔ	33	Ⓐ	Ⓑ	Ⓒ	Ⓓ	Ⓔ
9	Ⓐ	Ⓑ	Ⓒ	Ⓓ	Ⓔ	34	Ⓐ	Ⓑ	Ⓒ	Ⓓ	Ⓔ
10	Ⓐ	Ⓑ	Ⓒ	Ⓓ	Ⓔ	35	Ⓐ	Ⓑ	Ⓒ	Ⓓ	Ⓔ
11	Ⓐ	Ⓑ	Ⓒ	Ⓓ	Ⓔ	36	Ⓐ	Ⓑ	Ⓒ	Ⓓ	Ⓔ
12	Ⓐ	Ⓑ	Ⓒ	Ⓓ	Ⓔ	37	Ⓐ	Ⓑ	Ⓒ	Ⓓ	Ⓔ
13	Ⓐ	Ⓑ	Ⓒ	Ⓓ	Ⓔ	38	Ⓐ	Ⓑ	Ⓒ	Ⓓ	Ⓔ
14	Ⓐ	Ⓑ	Ⓒ	Ⓓ	Ⓔ	39	Ⓐ	Ⓑ	Ⓒ	Ⓓ	Ⓔ
15	Ⓐ	Ⓑ	Ⓒ	Ⓓ	Ⓔ	40	Ⓐ	Ⓑ	Ⓒ	Ⓓ	Ⓔ
16	Ⓐ	Ⓑ	Ⓒ	Ⓓ	Ⓔ	41	Ⓐ	Ⓑ	Ⓒ	Ⓓ	Ⓔ
17	Ⓐ	Ⓑ	Ⓒ	Ⓓ	Ⓔ	42	Ⓐ	Ⓑ	Ⓒ	Ⓓ	Ⓔ
18	Ⓐ	Ⓑ	Ⓒ	Ⓓ	Ⓔ	43	Ⓐ	Ⓑ	Ⓒ	Ⓓ	Ⓔ
19	Ⓐ	Ⓑ	Ⓒ	Ⓓ	Ⓔ	44	Ⓐ	Ⓑ	Ⓒ	Ⓓ	Ⓔ
20	Ⓐ	Ⓑ	Ⓒ	Ⓓ	Ⓔ	45	Ⓐ	Ⓑ	Ⓒ	Ⓓ	Ⓔ
21	Ⓐ	Ⓑ	Ⓒ	Ⓓ	Ⓔ	46	Ⓐ	Ⓑ	Ⓒ	Ⓓ	Ⓔ
22	Ⓐ	Ⓑ	Ⓒ	Ⓓ	Ⓔ	47	Ⓐ	Ⓑ	Ⓒ	Ⓓ	Ⓔ
23	Ⓐ	Ⓑ	Ⓒ	Ⓓ	Ⓔ	48	Ⓐ	Ⓑ	Ⓒ	Ⓓ	Ⓔ
24	Ⓐ	Ⓑ	Ⓒ	Ⓓ	Ⓔ	49	Ⓐ	Ⓑ	Ⓒ	Ⓓ	Ⓔ
25	Ⓐ	Ⓑ	Ⓒ	Ⓓ	Ⓔ	50	Ⓐ	Ⓑ	Ⓒ	Ⓓ	Ⓔ

Mathematical Reasoning

FOR SELECTIVE SCHOOL TESTS, OPPORTUNITY CLASS TEST AND PROBLEM SOLVING

Use pencil when filling out this sheet

Fill in the circle correctly				
●	B	C	D	E

If you make a mistake neatly cross it out and circle the correct response				
● (crossed out)	●	C	D	E

MULTIPLE CHOICE ANSWER SHEET

1	A	B	C	D	E
2	A	B	C	D	E
3	A	B	C	D	E
4	A	B	C	D	E
5	A	B	C	D	E
6	A	B	C	D	E
7	A	B	C	D	E
8	A	B	C	D	E
9	A	B	C	D	E
10	A	B	C	D	E
11	A	B	C	D	E
12	A	B	C	D	E
13	A	B	C	D	E
14	A	B	C	D	E
15	A	B	C	D	E
16	A	B	C	D	E
17	A	B	C	D	E
18	A	B	C	D	E
19	A	B	C	D	E
20	A	B	C	D	E
21	A	B	C	D	E
22	A	B	C	D	E
23	A	B	C	D	E
24	A	B	C	D	E
25	A	B	C	D	E
26	A	B	C	D	E
27	A	B	C	D	E
28	A	B	C	D	E
29	A	B	C	D	E
30	A	B	C	D	E
31	A	B	C	D	E
32	A	B	C	D	E
33	A	B	C	D	E
34	A	B	C	D	E
35	A	B	C	D	E
36	A	B	C	D	E
37	A	B	C	D	E
38	A	B	C	D	E
39	A	B	C	D	E
40	A	B	C	D	E
41	A	B	C	D	E
42	A	B	C	D	E
43	A	B	C	D	E
44	A	B	C	D	E
45	A	B	C	D	E
46	A	B	C	D	E
47	A	B	C	D	E
48	A	B	C	D	E
49	A	B	C	D	E
50	A	B	C	D	E